D1431335

I, TOO, AM AMERICA

I, TOO, AM AMERICA

A Book of Poems

By

LEONARD A. SLADE, JR.

For Anita and Bill, in Friendship!

Thank you for your support.

Leonard A. Slade Jr.

September 2018

XULON PRESS

Xulon Press
2301 Lucien Way #415
Maitland, FL 32751
407.339.4217
www.xulonpress.com

© 2018 by Leonard A. Slade, Jr.

All rights reserved solely by the author. The author guarantees all contents are original and do not infringe upon the legal rights of any other person or work. No part of this book may be reproduced in any form without the permission of the author. The views expressed in this book are not necessarily those of the publisher.

Printed in the United States of America.

ISBN-13: 9781545625613

Contents

Foreword

Recognizing that the power of the human community is its ability to appreciate and celebrate its diversity, as a spiritual thinker and humanistic writer Leonard A. Slade, Jr. thrives on the challenge always confronting the poet to perceive imaginatively the infinite possibilities of humanity and transform that perception into poetry that models courage, empowerment, and action. A poet, a professor, and a student of history for well over four decades, in his poetry Slade expresses the sense urgency he feels to impress on his readers as well as his students the importance of memory to the advancement of human culture and, in Whitmanesque terms, the celebration of the self as a means to improve the human condition for all. Indeed, his work amplifies the sensibility once expressed by Marianne Moore to the effect that "the poetic" "is a primal necessity"; Moore's position was later elaborated upon by two poets who Slade acknowledges as influences on his own verse: first, by Langston Hughes, who observed in his last years that "poetry is the human soul, entire, squeezed like a lemon or a lime, drop by drop into atomic words," and, then, by Gwendolyn Brooks, who believed her poems merited attention only to the extent that they demonstrated "life distilled."[1]

---

[1] *The Complete Prose of Marianne Moore*, ed. Patricia C. Willis (New York: Viking Press, 1986), p. 169; *The Collected Works of Langston Hughes: Essays on Art, Race, Politics, and World Affairs*, ed. Christopher C. De Santis (Columbia and London: University of Missouri Press, 2002), 9:408; Kevin Bezner, "A Life Distilled: An Interview with Gwendolyn Brooks" (1986),

I, Too, Am America

Raised in a close-knit large family in the segregated rural South in the years following World War II, in this latest collection Slade pays homage largely to those poets who have served as his cultural and intellectual models for the ideals they represent, but also to a number of academics and others whose representation of the American experience have provided this poet with ideals worthy of admiration and emulation. *I, Too, Am America* celebrates both the aesthetic debt Slade owes to Langston Hughes who coined the expression that provides the volume's title and the debt of freedom won through the heroic action and electric, if not atomic, language by those among the long train of poets, reformers, and patriots of the African-American experience that expressions such as Hughes's signal. In his earlier volumes of poetry Slade's emphasis invariably tended toward the personal and the autobiographical as represented by poems such as "Family – Glorious" and "Aunt Lizzie Pearl" written in commemoration of the centrality of family values to his growth as a child and, later, a poet, "Thank you, God" and "Prayer" written to acknowledge the comfort and efficacy of faith for those struggling to achieve genuine freedom in the pre- and post-Civil Rights era, and "Fire and Fury," "Racists," and "For my Forefathers" written to announce the poet's fierce dedication to never allowing America's destructive version of its own apartheid to be forgotten.[2] *I, Too, Am America* is Slade's extended tribute to those whose struggles as African-Americans have informed his own sense of poetic heritage and personal responsibility, and to those who, through their actions and

---

rpt. in *Conversations with Gwendolyn Brooks*, ed. Gloria Wade Gayles (University Press of Mississippi, 2003), p. 124.

[2] "Family – Glorious," (Leonard A. Slade, Jr., *Jazz After Dinner*, [Albany: State University of New York Press, 2006], pp. 46-47) and "Aunt Lizzie Pearl" (Leonard A. Slade, Jr., *I Fly Like a Bird*, [Winston-Derek Publishers, Inc.: Nashville, TN, 1992], p. 20); "Thank you, God" (Leonard A. Slade, Jr., *Triumph*, www.xulonpress.com, 2010, p. 55) and "Prayer" (Leonard A. Slade, Jr., *The Season*, www.xulonpress.com, 2011, p. 33); "Fire and Fury," (Leonard A. Slade, Jr., *The Whipping Song*, [Mellen Poetry Press: Lewiston/Queenston/Lampeter, 1993], p. 1), "Racists" (*Triumph*, p. 75), and "For my Forefathers" (*The Whipping Song*, p. 3).

beliefs—and regardless of their racial or ethnic origins—have shown him that Hughes's thesis is universal. Here, too, Slade writes out of the two threads of poetic sensibility that have informed his verses, which he earlier had announced in "Aims":

> Poetry should aim
>   Low for earthly things
> Lifting hearts
>   From depths of despair.
>
> Poetry should aim
>   High for stars
> Sending messages
>   Of love eternal.[3]

The importance of *I, Too, Am America* resides in its extraordinary historical sweep of poems that treat the emergence of a broad African-American consciousness from the early days of American nationhood, through the poet-bellum period, across the twentieth century, and then to the present; included also are poems that address the determination of public servants who transcended racial lines to eradicate the lingering hatred and darkness that led up to and finally advanced America's Civil Rights movement in the mid-twentieth century. This volume can easily serve as inaugural reading for an entire course that integrates history, social and political science, and literature as its subject. Indeed, among the eighty figures treated are the colonial America poet Phillis Wheatley (1754-84), the astronomer and naturalist Benjamin Banneker (1731-1806), as well as the nineteenth-century's most significant authors, abolitionists, orators, social activists and reformers, women's rights advocates, and educators: Sojourner Truth (c. 1797-1883), Harriet Tubman (1820-1913), Frederick Douglass (c. 1818-95), Booker T. Washington (1856-1915), Charles Chesnutt (1858-1932), George Washington Carver (early 1860s-1943),

---

[3] Leonard A. Slade, Jr., *Neglecting the Flowers* (New York: The McGraw-Hill Companies, Inc., 1997), p. 7.

W. E. B. Du Bois (1868-1963), James Weldon Johnson (1871-1938), Paul Laurence Dunbar (1872-1906), and Mary McLeod Bethune (1875-1955).

I, Too, Am America also celebrates twentieth-century American heroes whose respective legacies of fighting to eradicate racially driven oppression and gnawing poverty and to advance the cause of social justice emanates from their lives-as-lived and reflect the tenor our own time. Slade's contemporaries—including the present writer—will find writ large here not only the spirit acted upon by marchers and martyrs to advance the Civil Rights movement in the 1950s and 1960s, but also restores through the memories of those among us whose social consciences were shaped by the bullets of assassins aimed toward those in the advance guard of America's finally achieving promise of the democracy, the horrors of the Viet Nam War, and the egregious breaches of democratic principles for political gain that marred the opening years of our adulthood in the late 1960s and early 1970s. To address the challenge of those days, Slade re-invokes the aspirations of political and judicial leaders and writers who stood fast with America's ideals, including Presidents Franklin D. Roosevelt, John F. Kennedy, and Lyndon Johnson, Supreme Court Justice Thurgood Marshall, and, more recently, Barack Obama; modern writers in multiple genres such as Zora Neale Hurston, Richard Wright, Ralph Ellison, Alice Walker, Maya Angelou, Toni Morrison, Amiri Baraka, and Gwendolyn Brooks; and historians and cultural critics of the caliber of John Hope Franklin and Henry Louis Gates, Jr. Martyrs of the American Civil Rights movement are also present in poems dedicated to Martin Luther King, Jr. and Medgar Evers.

Interspersed among these poems and others not mentioned here are loving tributes by Slade to his family and respectful tributes to his academic colleagues, whose constancy provides strengthens the poet's own, especially, one must believe, as he takes on the pain and suffering of so many of his people in his art. Yet as even this poet, whose verses exude a spirit of hope against centuries' worth of seemingly insurmountable odds that confronted African-Americans, readers know that the aspirations of countless known and unknown Wheatleys, Tubmans, Carvers, Ellisons, Morrisons, and Kings have yet to be achieved.

There is no denying the passion out of which Leonard A. Slade, Jr. writes; neither is there any escape from the culture of inhumanity still advanced by those who argue that the injustice suffered by those whose burden it was to shoulder the labor and endure the insufferable demeaning of their human dignity in the making of America was merely a reflection of the values of their time. In truth, historical time as reflected across the poems gathered in *I, Too, Am America* is still at work in the America of our time. Taking on the mantle of the Black Lives Matter movement, Slade eulogizes Michael Brown, whose "hands were raised toward Heaven / When six bullets sent him back to earth / Where blood ran like water [and set] / The nation's soul on fire," and he counsels us that, although every generation may have its challenges and peculiar values, ours cannot be to countenance "race relations going backwards, / Ending in the grave."

Ronald A. Bosco
University at Albany, SUNY

I, too, sing America...
I, too, am America.
—Langston Hughes

PHILLIS WHEATLEY

Classical in her treatment of poetry,
She published poems
To protest racism and
The bad behavior of students.
Brilliant with her structure of poems
And thematic development.
Here was a scholar
Who showed the world
What a black person
Could do with the pen
In the 1700's and 1800's
When slaves were prevented
From reading and writing.
Here was a writer,
Here was a genius,
Here was a giant,
For the ages.

GEORGE MOSES HORTON

From Northampton County, North Carolina, a
slave labors on a farm;
he walks to the State University at Chapel Hill
writing love poems for students on weekends
to send home to their sweethearts,
money exchanged for the purchase of freedom.

Published poetry in newspapers,
books reflecting his genius
he studies Methodist hymns
how happy could readers be

when the Civil War ends
he travels to Philadelphia for respect
from the black bourgeoisie
books published for eternity
the whereabouts of his death
unknown.

JEAN-BAPTIST DU SABLE

Pioneer and entrepreneur
And settler in Chicago,
He bought land
And lived prosperously.
He spied for the British
But was jailed anyway.
He was a fur trapper
And a shrewd gentleman.
Chicago became our
wealthy memory of him.

BENJAMIN BANNEKER

He wrote a letter to Thomas Jefferson in 1791
Challenging his view that blacks were inferior to whites
Though sympathetic Jefferson was to black people,
Banneker appealed to him to re-evaluate his thinking
And reminded him that all are created
Equal by God in Heaven.
Banneker tells Jefferson to practice what
He wrote on human rights in the Declaration of
Independence.
Until Jefferson and all afterwards rid
themselves of prejudice
America would always have racial problems
Which are deeply rooted in our culture.
Banneker was a visionary.
Peace will never be in our land
Until all are free.

SOJOURNER TRUTH

She spoke with thunder
Let my people go.
She fought for women's rights,
Bore thirteen children
Who were sold into slavery.
Her mystical vision was to travel
America to speak the truth
About slavery and freedom.
She sang gospel songs
And interrupted meetings
Protesting slavery and women's subjugation.
She said no to male chauvinism
And yes to freedom for all.
She died whispering
"I'm free, thank God!
I'm free, thank God!"

ABRAHAM LINCOLN

He sucked a thumb in Kentucky,
where his father chopped wood
for warm evenings
in December. He wore old
clothes and walked barefoot
among lilacs in spring. And everywhere
he moved, Indiana and Illinois,
laughter filled the air

as young boys teased his height
and demeaned his clothes. No
child ever praised him,
and he for his suffering honored
her, all children thought small
of his future, except her
who read her Bible and loved him
as no other person could.

He studied by candlelight,
savoring words and defining dreams
for America. He was hungry for truth
and debated the pros and cons
of slavery. He promised a united country
but blood would taint freedom.
Brother against brother
sister against sister

blacks against whites
Northerners against Southerners –
they all fought for their cause.
Our father of freedom
bathed America with hope
and then was bathed himself
in cold blood.
Children cried.

ELIZABETH KECKLEY

I see Elizabeth Keckley working
As a seamstress for Abraham Lincoln,
Mary Todd being comforted by her,
A former slave suffering floggings,
Now sewing warm red clothes
For the restless First Lady.
Her mahogany body gracing
The White House, her voice sweet
With love in her heart,
She teaches The President
The beauty of Blackness,
The power of brotherhood.
I see a warrior,
I see a modiste,
I see a Saint
Singing in Heaven.

HARRIET TUBMAN

"The Moses of Her People"
Led hundreds out of bondage.
She was called stupid
During a brutal childhood.
She worked in the fields
And escaped slavery
To become "the conductor"
Of the Underground Railroad.
Several Northern abolitionists
Supported her cause.
She was a cook
And a nurse and a spy.
"The Moses of Her People"
Died loving freedom.

FREDERICK DOUGLASS

Like Frederick Douglass, I battle you,
stir your conscience, America,
so rich, with welfare and homelessness,
and crime galore, so much slavery now.

Like Douglass, I share biting truth, but
you open my heart, hoping for change, although
I smile at you through wrinkles of blood – you,
my sweet home, stir me to tears.

JOHN BROWN

The revolutionary's faith in freedom
     The power he shares;
The guns he carries for protection,
     He for some betrays.

His willingness kissing death,
     His words written in blood,
And actions speak for him,
     His heart knows truth.

But still he knows the future
     That freedom will come
For all who will make sacrifices
     The land must first soak in blood.

BOOKER T. WASHINGTON

He walked from West Virginia to Virginia
To earn a college degree at Hampton
Where he worked day and night.
He swept floors spotless.
For four years the college president
Observed his sound industry
And dedication to pure scholarship.
After graduation he taught school
Until the college president recommended him
To lead Tuskegee Institute to greatness.
He hired a famous scientist to head
The Agriculture Department;
He made national news with his research.
President Franklin D. Roosevelt praised him.
Philanthropists supported and admired
His vision for a better America.

LITTLEBERRY LANGFORD

I think of him every summer now;
1873 graduate of Hampton Institute who

taught school with fire and fervor.
Every year at the Family Reunion, his

name explodes with curiosity, as
he sleeps in his grave. And now

I appreciate this wordsmith who
studied Theology at Drew University

and preached in Canada and the Northeast
leaving his autobiography for ancestors.

Not a week passes I don't think of him;
teacher and preacher of words stretching

minds and touching human hearts.
He lives through his flesh and blood.

He prays daily in Heaven,
he reaches down to us with love.

He still dreams for us
he closes his eyes, singing.

PAUL LAURENCE DUNBAR

He received national recognition
writing about excruciating pain.
His parents lived as slaves,
Believing that one day his works
Would make him a man.
He befriended Frederick Douglass
Who recognized his greatness.
He mastered standard English
And authenticated black dialect.
Although frail he kept writing
He kept writing.
He kept writing.

CHARLES CHESNUTT

He wanted to be remembered
Not for his college presidency,
Not for his college degree,
Not for his mundane work
But for his **The Marrow of Tradition**
And for his **The House of Cedars**
Local in color,
Defying description,
Published for the ages.

W. E. B. Du Bois

Dr. Du Bois! you should be breathing now;
America needs you: some are children
Of crack and cocaine, AIDS, murders,
Crimes, street gangs, prostitution, and prisons.
Have changed our culture forever
Of eternal happiness. America suffers;
Speak to us, return please!
Your *Souls of Black Folk* was our hope.
Your voice was prophetic,
Changing like the seasons, predicting
Spring and winter between races,
Yet you sleep while we work another century.

SERGEANT HENRY JOHNSON

He believed in freedom
Fought for us,
Died in America's bosom.
He was black and beautiful,
Bold and the best
His heart was our love,
His beliefs were our future.
He gave us the world.
Selfless,
Visionary,
Spiritual.
His past was our history,
His dream was our present,
His life is in the Heavens.

A Tribute Inspired by Langston Hughes

'I've known rivers':
'I've known rivers' current 'as the world.'

'My soul grows deep like the rivers.'

I listened to Stokely Carmichael
      when furious fire heated cool air.
I shook hands with Martin Luther King, Jr.,
      before garbage cans in Memphis.
I heard shots in Dallas
      when John F. Kennedy waved at me.

'I've known rivers.'

I heard the drums of stomachs in New York,
      when welfare queens paraded the streets.
I danced to the melody of Diana Ross
      when Leontyne Price sang at the Met.
I read Sunday school lessons at home
      when Alice Walker wrote *The Color Purple.*

'I've known rivers.'

I bathed the body of a Rolls Royce
      when shacks cuddled me with love.
I plowed through books at Morehouse College
      when white men perused works at Harvard.
I moved into the mainstream
      a century after Huck and Jim journeyed down the
      Mississippi.

'My soul grows deep like the rivers.'

Langston Hughes – Princeton University

James Weldon Johnson

He taught blacks to
"Lift every voice and sing."
He created beauty in poetry
Rooted in a rich culture.
He taught creative writing at
Atlanta University where he
Contributed to the intellectual enlargement
Of all students' lives.
He kept telling us to
"March on till victory is won."
He lives in our hearts.
He stirs our souls.

COUNTEE CULLEN

Born of African ancestors,
Determined to be remembered.
He became our Black Keats,
Defining the lyricism of truth
And the power of beauty and goodness.
He wrote about the North and the South,
Used his NYU and Harvard training to
Sing with "lips that cold death kissed."

JEAN TOOMER

His publishing *Cane* immortalized
The power and beauty of his fiction
Poetry and drama written realistically.
School segregation in Georgia inspired
Him to tell the story of blacks
In America, the good and the ugly.
He heightened blacks' level of consciousness
About the problem of racial oppression
And poverty in our rich land.
Despite tragedy and perturbation
Blacks were determined to return to their roots
And not worship materialism, but only their God.
He told it all without worrying
About Fame or glory as a writer.
He ascended to the Heavens
Happy.

GEORGE WASHINGTON CARVER

He studied agriculture assiduously
And joined Booker T. Washington
At Tuskegee Institute
Where many uses of the
Peanut, sweet potato,
Pecan, and cotton
Would change the agrarian
Way of life forever.
The Royal Academy of England
Named him a Fellow.
The NAACP bestowed upon him
The Spingarn Medal.
Franklin Delano Roosevelt
Honored him with gratitude
And praise for
Work well done.
Here was a scholar,
Here was a researcher,
Here was a giant
Who changed America forever.

MARGARET WALKER

Her poetry was not just for her people
But for all people who read it
With supreme pleasure
And who experienced her excruciating
Pain. No one would dare
Plagiarize her novels or poems,
For some judge would reprimand.
She loved teaching and writing
And shared her gifts
With Richard Wright who
Would gain lasting fame.
She gave us Jubilee.
She reminisced about childhood days.
She spread literary gospel and verisimilitude
That still stir souls.

FRANKLIN D. ROOSEVELT

New York elected him Governor
But higher office was his fate.
He ran for U.S. President
When the Depression crippled
America with hunger and homelessness.
Banks closed and Americans
Begged for food and water.
Harvard prepared him to be
A national problem solver.
He toured the country promising
Better days ahead for thirteen
Years when the country suddenly lost him.
He helped Americans with food;
He put money in people's pockets,
People returned to work.
He fought a World War with might.
His greatness continues.

ELEANOR ROOSEVELT

Laughed at by relatives,
Called ugly by friends,
She buried her childhood
Memories and gave birth
To beauty and goodness.
She traveled all over the world
Determined to bring nations together,
Carving a document for
The now and our tomorrows.
She loved blacks and whites,
And stood alone for right.
We keep asking
"Why didn't you become
President of the United States?"
Your destiny was in the stars.
We dream your new world.

Robert L. Vann

His Virginia Union University
And University of Pittsburgh degrees
Prepared him for publishing and politics.
He supported Republican Presidents
And changed Party affiliation.
Franklin D. Roosevelt rewarded him.
The Pittsburgh Courier immortalized him.
He flies now with Republicans
And Democrats
In Heaven.

MELVIN B. TOLSON

He graduated from Lincoln University
And later taught at Wiley College
Where he coached the debating team.
He later earned a master's degree
From Columbia University where
He would write a thesis on
The Harlem Renaissance and begin
Writing Harlem Gallery and other poems.
He valued black racial pride
And kept writing an award-winning
Poem, "Dark Symphony," which
Was published in The Atlantic Monthly.
He wrote about the rise and fall
Of all civilizations with allusions
And linguistic and textual sophistication.
He challenged readers to
Drink deep of the well of creativity.
His students would win a national
Debate with a prestigious university.
He produced great debaters,
Poems rich and powerful.
"Oh, how can we forget?"

MAHATMA GANDHI

He studied Henry David Thoreau
And the principles of passive resistance.
He hungered for India's independence
Fasted until freedom rang.
His disciples followed him
As they had followed peace
Two thousand years earlier.
He traveled from city to city
Protesting injustice and
Demanding love and freedom.
His assassination changed
India forever.
Even Great Britain
Celebrated freedom ringing.

RICHARD WRIGHT

Deserted by his father when he was five
He stayed with different relatives
And later made an orphanage his home.
He began writing in Memphis,
Then moved to Chicago
And later to New York City.
His schools did not encourage him.
He borrowed books from a library,
Forging a request from a white borrower.
He had experienced it all:
Poverty and racial prejudice,
Little education and an unstable family.
His novel <u>Native Son</u> was a masterpiece.
He moved to Paris, France
Where he was treated like a man,
Where he died after writing
"The sirens and the bells....
And the screams had filled the air."

ZORA NEALE HURSTON

Her father wanted whippings
for her so that she could
live safely in a white world.
Her mother wanted freedom
for her so that she could jump
to the moon and write
her novels and stories
about beauty and ugliness,
good and evil in a segregated world.
She studied and wrote,
She traveled and published.
Here was a revolutionary
scribbling truths about
blackness and whiteness,
Here was a genius
Castigated for her womanhood,
Here was a literary giant
Celebrated forever for the power of her words.

I, Too, Am America

CLAUDE McKAY

He sang songs of Jamaica
With ungrammatical profundity.
He studied the English Romantic poets
And used them as models to
Write social protest poems.
Menial jobs did not embarrass him.
Racism in America perturbed him.
He traveled the world looking
For the right philosophy of life.
He found freedom **A Long Way from Home.**

RALPH BUNCHE

Born in the slums
He later studied at the University of California
And at Harvard University.
He became an expert on race relations
And shared his knowledge at Howard.
He traveled the world
Carrying out diplomatic missions.
He resolved the Arab-Israel conflict.
He received the Nobel Peace Prize
And the Presidential Medal of Freedom.
This black man
This professor extraordinaire
This Prince of Peace
Loved our world so.

MARY MCLEOD BETHUNE

She picked cotton until
Scotia College called her for training.
The president of Bethune-Cookman College
And the founder-president
Of the National Council of Negro Women,
She created the Black Cabinet
Of the New Deal.
She taught the work ethic.
She taught Black pride
She mentored Langston Hughes.
She predicted a future
That could make us
Healthy and whole.

JAMES BALDWIN

He wrote it all
Beginning at age fourteen,
Preaching in the pulpit,
Telling it all on the mountain,
Conflicting with his stepfather.
His books and essays showed
Him strutting his stuff,
Burning with truth,
Sharing family joys and sorrows.
We now know his name.
Oh, if he would only talk now!

THE REVEREND PAUL BISHOP OF NORTH CAROLINA

His five churches permitted
him to preach the Word
and to persuade parents to send
their children to college.
No matter how well children
sang and prayed in God's House,
during and after the Depression,
he would admonish parents
to make sacrifices and to send
their flesh and blood to a
private or public institution.
Although churches were
small and members were
common laborers and good farmers,
children and parents heard
the visionary pastor.
Before and after his
death hundreds earned
college degrees.
Others earned professional
and doctoral degrees,
became lawyers and
doctors and teachers and
professors all over the country.
The pastor's words affected lives,
changed communities and
altered the culture of
a people forever.

RALPH ELLISON

Novelist, you write with clarity and grace.
Powerful symbols, they are rich
meanings of life. Blackness permeates
each page, and I feel humble,
for you are existential, writer
of truths, writer of objectivity,
writer of transcendentalism, from whose words
I have given birth to poetry.
You are the master writer of journeys,
writer from Oklahoma, writer of hope.
I admire you, pray for your soul,
remember your profound lectures,
Harlem who welcomed your characters,
who loved black revolution,
who didn't know death,
Harlem who housed the oppressed of the world,
whose culture I worship,
for knowing your life rooted in love
immortalizes hungry humanity.

ETHERIDGE KNIGHT

He loved juke joints and poker games.
He loved verbal performances and great oratory.
He robbed others and served prison time.
Gwendolyn Brooks and Dudley Randall
Praised his prison poetry.
Sonia Sanchez separated from him
Because of his drug addiction.
No matter!
He was the "Flute of Black Lovers"
Who was "buried in the dust
Of marching feet."

JOHN F. KENNEDY

He finished Harvard
And published <u>Profiles in Courage</u>.
Receiving a Pulitzer Prize.
Massachusetts loved his youth,
Elected him as their Senator.
His family wealth blessed him
During the Depression
When his father predicted
The crash of the Stock Market
And acted wisely for financial gain.
He ran for President of the United States
Whipping Nixon with his eloquence
Asking us what we could do for America,
Not what America could do for us.
He admitted his failure with the Bay of Pigs
But humbly celebrated his courage
To make Krushchev turn back his
Ships headed to Cuba.
Conflict between blacks and whites
In the South challenged
His national leadership.
In the decade of the 1960's.
Malcolm and King
Had a rendezvous with death.
John and Robert would join them.
Americans sang,
"Let us march on 'til victory is won."

John F. Kennedy – 1964 Warren Commission Report

I, Too, Am America

Lyndon Johnson

He was one proud Texan
Larger than life.
He loved family
And relished politics.
He wanted to make
Our society great.
The Vietnam War tainted his name.
Oh, his Lady Bird supported him,
America now appreciates him,
A president for all seasons.

THURGOOD MARSHALL

His grandfather was a slave,
His mother was a master teacher.
He studied at Lincoln and Howard,
Later working for the NAACP.
He loved our civil rights.
Brown v. Board of Education
Internationalized him.
Lyndon Johnson distinguished him
As an associate justice
Of the U. S. Supreme Court.
The U. S. Justice System
Will never know of his likes again.

Mordecai Johnson

Some posed questions. You are thunder--
We questioned and questioned-- you answered cogently,
Sharing knowledge. For the university on the hill,
Where students come for intellectual food,

Taking notes on your lectures,
Watching you move all over the stage,
Hungry for truth and justice
In the world of trouble;

And you, who know Africa and Asia,
North America and South America,
Did get a formal global education-- yes!

All because your disciples at Howard,
Which became the capstone of education,
Your graduates entered the world with fire.

LORRAINE HANSBERRY

Langston Hughes inspired her
Play's title, <u>A Raisin in the Sun</u>.
The reputation of her publications
Did not diminish the power
Of her masterpiece.
She knew motherhood and sisterhood.
Brotherhood between the races
Became one of her themes.
Racism and sexism did
Not take a back seat.
She dreamed of freedom
For her people in all
Neighborhoods. Her dipped
Pen revealed truths
That aroused the consciousness
Of a divided America.

BARBARA JORDAN

She studied at Boston University
Where she mastered legal analysis
And perfect debating skills.
She would serve people well
In the Lone Star State
Where her voice boomed
For respect and action.
Even world leaders yielded
To her oratory skills abroad and
In the Congress of the United States.
She frequently quoted The Constitution.
Here was a scholar,
Here was a force who wielded power
And helped oust
A President of the United States.

Paule Marshall

Her love for Caribbean culture
Gave the world a Brownstones novel.
Her mother taught her the power
Of words and what they can do
In a world rife with conflict.
Her storyteller skills were awarded
With a Guggenheim and Ford Foundation Grant.
Her sweet demeanor and softspoken manner
Projected humility and goodness.
Her religion was kindness
That electrified communities.

WALTER N. RIDLEY

When it is ours, excellence, the best,
this quality and noble idea, needed as a value
in hearts and heads, schools and colleges, now;
when minds think and truth flows
like a pristine river, and knowledge is imparted
like diamond dew at sunrise;
when courses are history and art,
mathematics and science, literature and music,
an organic whole, and more:
the scholar, the teacher, the educator
structuring a curriculum and a life,
visioning an institution where learning is loved,
ignorance loathed, here.
This cultured gentle one,
wealthy with books and dreams,
this intellectual shall be remembered,
not with brick buildings,
not with gratitude and tributes
and plaques of gold alone,
but with students matured beyond college,
nurturing their lives, transforming a universe
needed now.

Medgar Evers

Born and educated in Mississippi,
He studied law and
Became active in civil rights.
He traveled night and day
Pleading for freedom.
Though he was cut down
In his driveway
His truth kept
Marching on.

MARTIN LUTHER KING, JR.

Year after
    year my
        friends remember King
            for his causes—

freedom and justice
    love, hope, and change
        needed now
        Communion and Prayer;

come, King!
    Heaven! Send him,
        his spirit
            to the bowels of the earth

to cleanse,
    coercing racists
        to vomit their evil
            from the past and present

purify souls, renew the earth
    we must remember King,
        police dogs, cold blood,
            black children bombed,

The Mississippi Burning,
    and how bullets
        find apostles and presidents
        and kings;

we must remember
    Montgomery and Memphis,
        the beginning and end,

we must remember
    we must remember
        we must remember
            The Dream.

MLK – USA Today

I, Too, Am America

ALICE WALKER

Born to sharecroppers
She learned hard work
And valued education.
Registering voters for power,
She commenced writing truth,
Teaching literature and writing,
Novels and poetry and essays.
Transcending violence and cruelty,
She triumphed over battles,
Telling her story that liberated
All women winning the Pulitzer Prize
For her telling it all.

JOSEPH JENKINS

We profited that this brilliant professor
By his love of students (undergraduates and graduates)
Brought out the best in them personally and
professionally,
Tickled their intellect with critical skills and
deep thinking,
Refused to permit anyone to treat primer subjects
But insisted on depth and breadth and power of
discussion,
Demonstrating his Phi Beta Kappa training
And Harvard University graduate degree.
He pushed and pushed students to their limit
To be their best producing master's and Ph.D. students
Who became distinguished professors and chief
administrators
In the public and private sector with lucrative salaries.
There worked the scholar; his voracious reading,
There he labored in the academy daily and on
weekends, too,
Teaching and preaching the power and beauty
of language.
Souls have toiled, inspired by his pure teaching
And love of learning for joy and peace and hope,
Yes with fire and fervor and passion for scholarship,
He baptized his disciples with cold water
Indifferent to maudlin feelings or personal
sentimentality
But objectifying philosophical and literary ideas
Making them relevant for the real world
Preparing solid citizens for the bad and the ugly
As well as the good and the beautiful and the light;
Though he is gone now to be with celestial stars,
We live through him from old days to new
Building earth and heaven
Committed to becoming him,
We work, we think, we move the world.

I, Too, Am America

CORAGREENE JOHNSTONE

Give me good memories, says the poet,
Give me free deconstruction;
I can't take your word for it, or
What you interpret.
Call on your obsequious "pets"
Who want good grades:
Your formal training, your being petty,
How can you rest in your grave?

You were unfair, unless
Everyone agreed with you –
How did you get your doctorate?
Broaden your mind?
You lowered grades
Of iconoclasts,
Of those who questioned,
Philosophers hungry for truth.

Read books in your grave –
You book worm
With your pedantic brilliant mind,
Dedicated once to your students,
Always willing to help them,
Courageous in sharing your knowledge
No matter how controversial –
You sleep peacefully immune to poetic criticism.

ELEGY FOR THERMAN B. O'DANIEL

I remember his voice, rich and golden;
And his urbane manner, majestic as a king;
And how, once meeting, a smile leaped for us,
And he thundered beliefs about journals and words
And how they last.
We sang, too, his melodies
And dreamed,
Our leafs turning to poems and stories;
Our songs tremble their criticism now.

He kindled an eternal flame
That burns hearts, young and old,
And sacrificed twilight years for stars,
And enjoyed the sunrise and sunsets.

If only we could assure him now
That his work reaped harvests for all seasons,
The fruits of his labors save the world.

I, Too, Am America

Maya Angelou

Brilliant. Beautiful.
Gracious. Grand.
Radiant. Rare.
She burns us with fire furious,
Sings us with pain and pleasure.
Her words are our power.
Her presence is our peace.
Her voice is our victory.
Eternity is her home.

Maya Angelou – NY Post

I, Too, Am America

MANDELA

Steel
Hard-boned.
Logic-minded.

He has the universe on his shoulders.
We admire. We see a man.
The man making us safe and protecting our world
and giving us tomorrows.

And with quiet strength and a lion's courage
Mandela imprisoned and demanding
freedom for us.

He sacrifices –
his years and life
for our flesh and blood.

RICHARD BARKSDALE

A scholar left us gifts.

He was a marriage partner.
He was a tender father.
He was a spiritual giant.

He wrote the "Bible" in black literature.
His intellect is
        the wealth of the world.

His work yearns in desire
        a completeness.

His criticism stimulates tomorrows,
        for thousands of "disciples" leading.

His work was gold.

May he sleep among the stars.
May we work an eternal moon.

CLAY SIMPSON

Think of a black American you know,
alive and active, count
his deeds – his fruit –
ripening with age;
or a pillar in the community
a husband and father first,
a velvety politician
skilled in laboring
the medicine man and comedian
curing the blues and absorbing pain;
or the benefactor for the young,
a listener of tall tales,
and a giant defying the years –
unpretentious and unassuming,
responsive to human needs –
Dr. Simpson,
accept gratitude deserved,
honeyed with words.

Andrew Baskin

Wealthy, a little shy at times
is why we love him:
editing poetry and articles,
brilliant mind always thinking,
improving arts and humanities
on the printed page of journals,
books produced to last, too.
Indifferent to praise,
humility characterizes him, oh,
and dedication with sweat and tears,
with joy and fulfillment:
I admire him, all the qualities he exudes
(like an intellectual giant, inimitable).

HELEN MARSHALL CALDWELL

Brilliant.
Classy.
Dedicated.

She was a loyal wife.
We admired. We see a sweet mother.
The sweetness making the soul noble,
developing minds to the maximum.

And under her Vice Chancellorship
Elizabeth City State became nationally-ranked.
Here lives an intellectual giant

Regal with style and grace
a work celebrated that
changed the world.

Her name immortalized
Her whole being

made Divine.

KAREN R. HITCHCOCK

now President of
the University at Albany

of the State University
of New York

containing a microcosm of
a macrocosm

of higher education
changing the world

forever

WILLIAM SETTLE, SR.

Coworkers considered him kind and gentle,
always willing to work hard for a living.
Church members considered him a Christian soldier,
Always depending on God for help and strength.
Friends considered him sincere and amiable,
Always treating others as he wanted to be treated.
His children considered him their hero,
Always there for them in their hour of need.
His wife considered him a spiritual giant,
Always willing to take the high road to Heaven.

RAYMOND M. BURSE

According to the University's needs,
    this tall black man, Rhodes Scholar
        (at a mahogany desk not separate from the
            rest of his cohorts);

these ardent administrators
    and this erudite faculty and

these curious students
    with their books and fertile minds

have come willingly
    to follow this President
        dedicated to them
            (and a living organism).

It is here
    (since learn we must),
        made sacred by a higher being,

This leader's co-workers
    are determined in their efforts
        (yes, intellectual and spiritual),

as must be in this public place.

This family is one, a microcosm,
    here in time.
        The Chief,
            his head bowed to share

his vision,
>works alone
>>and with us. While
>>>our eyes are closed, late
>>>the Chief works,
>>>>turning to papers and what not

at this University. The students
>and we are satisfied.
>>The President and we
>>are one
>>(a whole must we be).

ROBERTA HALL SLADE

You who loved much – unconditionally –
Yet survived crucifixion for moral principles,
Challenged thinkers in meetings, bless them –
Earned respect from the intelligentsia,

Intolerant of ignorance and stupidity: Roberta, listen!
O Darling, gifted musician, your music so beautiful
On the organ and piano supplemented
With your melodious singing;

The uneducated love your sounds,
The suffering you bring to art
Needs no explanation, giving birth
to compassion and joy –

Winter dies and spring comes.
Tears soak all souls.

ELIZABETH LANGFORD SLADE

picking cotton on
a cold day blisters
decorated her black fingers
in the fields

She crawled on her knees
until the sun bowed
to her. Eight children
planted beneath the stars
The earth felt good to her.

You can see her now
a parched face and folded hands
she kneels in a different place
drinking blood and eating bread
at the altar

Comforted white gloves feel good to her
waving to touch the sky
hymns fill the air
They feel good to her
they feel good to her

HENRY LOUIS GATES, JR.

He knew Piedmont, West Virginia,
Before he loved Yale and Cambridge.
He researched and published
His way to Cornell and Duke,
Stopping at Harvard
Where he showed more love,
Touched more lives
And gave more global education.
His awards defied description.
His writings burned the world.

I, Too, Am America

AUGUST WILSON

He left our world too soon
But shared with us his wealth
Of literary treasures that
Remain hidden in all hearts.
He destroyed fences and walls,
Played the piano for lessons
And told us who had come and gone.
His two Pulitzer Prizes
Validated his perfect craft.
His plays were performed on stage,
In movies with Denzel Washington
And Charles Dutton and Viola Davis.
His words pierced heavy hearts
And kissed sweet souls.

VINCENT O'LEARY

He recognized all cultures
And motivated his university to respect them:
Their similarities and differences,
Their hopes and dreams.
His faculty reflected global values
And his students became intellectual giants,
Entering the world after graduation,
Prepared to make a difference
In the quality of all lives
For the survival of our humanity.

CARL M. HILL

He prepared himself with learning
And living and worshipping ideals
That defied anyone's description.
Suave and urbane, erudite and patient,
He loved excellence and built colleges
By hiring the best minds
With whole hearts
Who could assist him with his cause.
Ivy League trained from Cornell
He was secure being one of the top
Inimitable chemists in the United States
And Canada. Here was an
Administrator, here was a scholar
Who made colleges powerful universities
For the structuring of a better America.
For the triumph of a Holy Spirit.

Nikki Giovanni

When she gives her commentary
about the rightness and
wrongness of America,
when she reads her
poetry about family
and friends and students,
when she teaches her English
classes at Virginia Tech
and challenges students
to create change in America
by building hearts in communities,
then the world gets better,
and the offering of peace
and enlightenment move
the world.

Nikki Giovanni – TheCreativeIndependent.com

I, Too, Am America

TONI MORRISON

When I moved to Albany, New York
And settled into my palatial office
In the Department of Africana Studies
I later met you in the Humanities Building
Where you invited me to chat with you.
You had just won the Pulitzer Prize
And received international praise for your
Prose sprinkled with clarity and grace.
You greeted me with humility and charm.

You cultivated genuine friendship with me.
You volunteered to give a free lecture
In my African-American Literature class
And expressed regret that you would not
Be staying at the University to teach.
Your greater destiny was to teach at
Princeton University where you received the
Nobel Prize in Literature from Sweden.
Years later I met you at MLA
And chatted with you about Albany.
You moved intellectuals with your fire
And brought revolution in letters to our world.

JOEL WISE WALLACE

When I was a graduate student I learned humility,
entered class ignorant of salient facts
in English and American Literature.
I saw him come to the room to teach
content that would be on Ph.D. Prelims.
Every night I studied for my master's degree,
determined that he would not yell at me
for not knowing copious facts and literary criticism.

I had possibilities he said
as he demonstrated his Ivy League
Ph.D. training from Columbia University,
and showed me how to write a Master's Thesis
so that I would one day
write a dissertation
without worrying about its quality.
I earned the M.A. in English at age 23
and later the Ph.D. at age 30,
indebted to an intellectual giant
who had predicted my future.

I, Too, Am America

Amiri Baraka

Words became his weapons
Destroying his freedom
To exaggerate and fictionalize.
His poetry offended
Those who worried about truth
And exalted others
Who valued the power of creativity.
His Poet Laureate position
Stripped him of his title
But his words remained his weapons
After he chewed worms in his grave.

GWENDOLYN BROOKS

Your stately stroll toward me
    kindles a flame of poetic fire.
Your coal blackness and wine blood
    increase your strength
    and inordinate beauty.
Your laughter hides historical pain.

You are life celebrated!

You are the Mother of Blackness
    and Ethnicity and Majesty.
You share your power with the Earth:
We must learn the strength of your love.
Your affection is the base for our being.

You have known suffering and sacrifice
    and oppression and strength.
An African King shares his need for you
    from afar.
Your Blackness must permeate the Universe.

YOU ARE!

I, Too, Am America

Gwendolyn Brooks – Art Shay for Colorado State University

RONALD HARMON BROWN

I heard from newsmen you may be flying
        over a mountain near Bosnia.

Gusty winds send torrents of rain
        and now I worry in the dark on my knees.

Bolts of lightning strike a big bird
        but my dream tonight will be pleasant.

When morning comes, I wake to learn
        a nightmare of you burned and broken
        my heart heavy.

Patricia Neal

The white Federated Church at Martha's Vineyard
Celebrated her life with laughter and tears.
She would leave family and friends.
Her brown coffin kept her body warm.
Sunflowers draped her wooden casket.
Ministers read Scripture about the power of love.
One speaker quoted John Keats:
Her beauty was a joy forever.
"Just a Closer Walk with Thee"
And "Amazing Grace" were sung for the Heavens.
At the end of the funeral program,
She received a standing ovation.
The curtain on her famous life closed.

John Hope Franklin

<u>From Slavery to Freedom</u>
Caught our attention.
Fisk and Harvard
Trained him with purity.
Over 30 colleges and universities
Would give him honorary doctorates.
Black colleges and universities
Hired him to teach wisely.
The University of Chicago and Duke
Lured him away.
His books and articles
Institutionalized him
In academics worldwide.

Ruthe Sheffey

Morgan State University nurtured her
Intellectually as Zora kept
Speaking to her about
Black people's human condition.
Langston visited her
Early in the morning for coffee
And Arna dined with her for lunch.
She taught the power of their literature.
Her national leadership positions
Did not keep her from learning
But kept her serving her people,
And all who shared her dream
To make our troubled world
Better than we found it.
She lives.
She lives,
She lives
Within our souls.

DONNA AKIBA SULLIVAN HARPER

Oh Akiba, Akiba, how do you do it?
You intellectualize the power of Langston Hughes
And publish to glowing reviews.
Your leadership earns you accolades
Your Distinguished Professorship
Validated your accomplishments.
Oh Akiba, Akiba, how do you do it?
God must have anointed you
With His grace and goodness.

MICHAEL BROWN

He left home to run an errand
At night when white subjects
Patrolled the neighborhood for safety.
His hands were raised toward Heaven
When six bullets sent him back to earth
Where blood ran like water.
The nation's soul was on fire,
Blacks protesting injustice
And some whites gleeful of the destruction
Of people who represented progress
In race relations going backwards,
Ending in the grave.

FREEMAN A. HRABOWSKI, III

He fought as an Illini
Earning the Ph.D. degree.
He became the university president
And challenged intellectuals with
Perfect leadership skills.
Among America's 10 Best College Presidents
According to <u>Time Magazine</u>,
He became one among 100 influential
People in the world.
Here is a scholar,
Here is a giant,
A mover and shaker of the universe.

GEORGE PHILIP

Amidst the pressures,
the verbal wars ready.
then he made hard decisions.
suppose he had been overlooked
to be university president?
before the budget ax fell?
I suppose the institution
would have bled profusely
not literally.
there are millions of people
who have now heard of the
university.
but here as a man I know
that he got through
the world of times
past faculty deaths.
increased our endowment
through darkness
and gave me hope
in this better place.
even the fat cut from the
financial gut of the university
making us lean and efficient.
I was glad they gave Philip
an ax,
he gave me powerful words,
encouraged me to publish widely
those evaluated truths about
deadwood faculty
in our world,
performing "abortions" on
new faculty arrivals,
I held on,
my ignorant self
preparing the praise of an
intellectual giant always
my brother.

Barack Obama

After such campaigns – what results?
What demarcation of votes? (to find
Among some regions rebelliousness that
Frightens freedom achieved based on merit.)

The Vision of America.
Model of rainbow coalitions:
Model of our desired equality:
Even the bloody history of our suffering.

We see rights ancestors died for.
We seek Paradise here: flowers, sunlight,
Clouds, the rain for growth and harvest
In this new century of all colors.

We seek morning stars.
A triumph of noble spirit.
We see our gifts and our leader.
Redeemed America. And Obama.

Barack Obama – biography.com

References

<u>African American Literature: Voices in a Tradition</u>. Austin, Texas: Holt, Rhinehart and Winston, Inc. (1992).

Low, W. Augustus, Virgil Clift. (Editors.) (1981). <u>Encyclopedia of Black America</u>. New York, New York: McGraw-Hill, Inc.

Slade, Jr., Leonard A. (2010). <u>Sweet Solitude</u>. Albany, New York: State University of New York Press.

I, Too, Am America

Acknowledgments

I am grateful to Dr. George Hendrick, Professor Andrew Baskin, Editor James Peltz, Professor Oscar Williams, Jr., and Professor Allen Ballard for their powerful words of encouragement, and to Martha's Vineyard, where some of these poems were written.

The sacrifice Roberta Hall Slade made in adjusting to my absence when I was hiding to write poetry is appreciated more than she will ever know.

About the Author

Leonard A. Slade, Jr. earned the bachelor's degree in English from Elizabeth City State University of the University of North Carolina System, the M.A. degree in English from Virginia State University, and the Ph.D. degree in English from the University of Illinois at Urbana-Champaign, where he graduated as the Edmund J. James Scholar in English. After receiving the doctorate, he did postdoctoral work at the University of Ghana in West Africa. He has taught at Kentucky State University, where he was Chair of the Division of Literature, Languages, and Philosophy and Dean of the College of Arts and Sciences; the University at Albany (SUNY), where he served as Director of the Humanistic Studies Doctoral Program and of the Master of Arts in Liberal Studies Program; Union College (Adjunct Professor); Skidmore College (Adjunct Professor); and RPI (Adjunct Professor). He is now Professor of Africana Studies, Adjunct Professor of English, Collins Fellow, and Citizen Academic Laureate at the University at Albany (SUNY).

He has published book reviews in *The Courier Journal*, *The Lexington Herald-Leader*, and the *CLA Journal*. He has also published articles in the *U.S. News and World Report*, *The English Journal: Publication of the National Council of Teachers of English*, *Emerge Magazine*, and *Education Next: Journal of Opinion and Research at Harvard University*. His poetry has appeared in *Essence Magazine, The Black*

Scholar, The Kentucky Poetry Review, The CLA Journal, The Zora Neale Hurston Forum, and *The Griot: Journal of the Southern Conference on African American Studies,* among other journals. The author of twenty-six books, including twenty-one books of poetry, Slade has received a number of national awards for his work. He has studied with Pulitzer Prize winners Stephen Dunn and Donald Justice.

CPSIA information can be obtained
at www.ICGtesting.com
Printed in the USA
FFHW01n0008040718
47318709-50344FF